WRITING A STATE REPORT

Written by John and Patty Carratello

Illustrated by Anna Chelton

We would like to give special thanks to Corinne Coombs and Michael Wirthlin for their ideas and interest in this book.

My State Report

Teacher Created Resources

Teacher Created Resources
6421 Industry Way
Westminster, CA 92683
www.teachercreated.com

ISBN: 978-1-55734-162-4

©1989 Teacher Created Resources
Reprinted, 2014

Made in U.S.A.

The classroom teacher may reproduce the materials in this book and/or CD for use in a single classroom only. The reproduction of any part of this book and/or CD for other classrooms or for an entire school or school system is strictly prohibited. No part of this publication may be transmitted or recorded in any form without written permission from the publisher with the exception of electronic material, which may be stored on the purchaser's computer only.

WRITING A STATE REPORT
Table of Contents

TO THE TEACHER

Writing a State Report is the book you will need to help your students complete a research paper on one of the fifty states.

The book begins with materials to aid your students in the research phase of report writing. An orientation to the library, the construction of bibliography materials, notecards, and footnotes, as well as the use of reference materials are introduced (or reviewed) in this section.

The remainder of *Writing A State Report* gives the student a step-by-step format for the creation and construction of their individual reports. Also included in this section are ideas for projects to accompany state reports, evaluation of the report experience, and a classroom project sharing activity.

We know you will find this book to be a valuable resource for you and your students when STATE REPORT time comes to your classroom!

WHAT IS RESEARCH?

When you want to know more about a subject, what do you do? _____

_____

_____

_____

_____

You RESEARCH!

Research *is an investigation. The idea behind research is to find out all the facts you can about the subject you are interested in.*

    * Circle the sources you **could** use to research facts.

encyclopedia	television	textbook
person	newspaper	yourself
magazine	almanac	non-fiction book
computer	video	atlas

A RESEARCH paper is a
PAPER that gives information
you have learned. You can learn
facts for your research paper
from all of the sources listed
above! Did you circle them all?

   yes   no

REQUEST LETTER

A valuable way to obtain information for your state report is to write a request letter to the tourist office in the state you have chosen.

In your letter, ask for specific information, such as a recent state map, census statistics, recreational points of interest, state resources, and so forth. Remember to be clear about what you need.

This form of research will give you current information about your state. You may also receive usable pictures for your report, in the form of pamphlets and brochures.

You will need to write your request letter as soon as possible. It may take weeks for you to receive any information in answer to your request.

Be sure to use business letter format, block or indented. Check with your teacher for the preferred format. Remember to be neat and to the point when you write.

Sample of Block Style

```
                                    6 Fall Street
                                    Williamsport, Indiana 47993
                                    February 10, 20__


Wyoming Travel Commission
I-25 at College Drive
Cheyenne, WY 82002-0660

Dear Sir or Madam:

Write the information you are requesting in the main body of
your letter.  Be concise.


                                    Sincerely yours,

                                    Your signature
                                    Your printed name
```

After you have received information from the tourist office, send an acknowledgment of thanks.

RESEARCH USING THE INTERNET

Encourage students to use a variety of resources as they search for state information. For students and teachers, the Internet provides a wealth of research material at their fingertips. As with any Internet-related activities in the classroom, follow school/district policy regarding Internet usage.

Use the following information to direct students to some of the best kid-friendly search engines.

1. **Google**™—Just type your topic and click "Google Search." If you want to narrow your search, go to the bottom of the page and click on "Search within results." Then type your qualifying topic into the new box and get a much more specific group of sites.

   http://www.google.com

2. **Yahooligans!**®—This site is specifically designed for kids ages 8–14. You can search by keywords or browse through categories.

   http://www.yahooligans.com

3. **AltaVista**—Search by keywords or use the directory. This engine also uses Boolean searches.

   http://www.altavista.com

4. **Ask Jeeves for Kids**™—Type your question and click on "ask."

   http://www.ajkids.com

A good tutorial on using search engines, called *Seven Steps Toward Better Searching,* can be found at the following website:

http://edweb.sdsu.edu/WebQuest/searching/sevensteps.html

There are many places your students can get pen pals or e-pals. Have the students write to a classroom (or individual students) from each state and compare culture, weather, geography, etc. The following websites provide information on obtaining e-mail addresses and/or e-pals.

1. **e-PALS Classroom Exchange**—This is a great place to get free e-mail accounts for the students in your class.

   http://www.epals.com/

2. **Teaching.com**—This site is another location where teachers can find e-mail accounts for their students.

   http://www.teaching.com/keypals/

LIBRARY ORIENTATION

The library in your school or town will be a key place to go to research for your state report. In order to make your library work for you, you need to know what resources are available and how to get and use them.

Do you know where these things are located in your library? Check the box if you know

- ☐ card catalog
- ☐ non-fiction
- ☐ history
- ☐ encyclopedia
- ☐ general works
- ☐ copy machine
- ☐ atlas books
- ☐ social science
- ☐ check out area

The card catalog is a cabinet of small file drawers in the library. You can find a card for each book in the library in the card catalog.

Books can be filed in three different ways in the card catalog:

1. By the *author's* last name
2. By the *title* of the book
3. By the *subject* of the book

Once you have found a book in the card catalog, you need to write the call number on a piece of paper, along with the author's name and/or book title.

The call number is a group of numbers and letters printed on the card catalog card and on the spine of the book. Knowing this number and where the number identifications are in the library will lead you to your book.

REMEMBER, IF YOU HAVE A QUESTION, ASK YOUR TEACHER OR LIBRARIAN. THEY WANT TO HELP!

BIBLIOGRAPHY CARDS

Bibliography cards *are small cards that are used to record information about the resources you use for your report.* When writing them, the author's last name is first, titles are underlined, and article names are in quotation marks. Here are some samples for you to use or copy.

ENCYCLOPEDIA

title: _____

author's name (if given): _____
topic in encyclopedia: " _____"

volume number or letter: _____
publishing location: _____

publishing company: _____
copyright date: _____
pages of useful information: _____
total pages: _____

PERIODICAL

author: _____
article title: " _____"

periodical title: _____

volume number: _____
date of periodical: _____

pages of useful information: _____

total pages: _____

BOOK

author: _____
title: _____
publishing location: _____

publishing company: _____

copyright date: _____
call number: _____
pages of useful information: _____

total pages: _____

INTERVIEW

name of interviewee: _____

interview location: _____

interview date: _____
interview time: _____
name of interviewer: _____

NOTECARDS

As you research sources for your report, you will need to take notes on the information you find. Good note taking helps to make a good report.

Remember these things as you take your notes.

☆ Take notes on notecards. You may buy index cards or cut your own. Notecards are good to take notes on because you can easily shuffle your notes around to be in the best order.

☆ Try not to copy word for word from what you've read. Write your notes in your OWN words. If you take your notes in incomplete sentences, when you write your report, more of the words will have to be your own!

☆ If you do copy from your source, put quotation marks around what you copy.

☆ Write the source you use for the information on each notecard.

☆ Write one idea on each notecard. Don't try to write too much on a card.

☆ Write a heading on each notecard to match your table of contents.

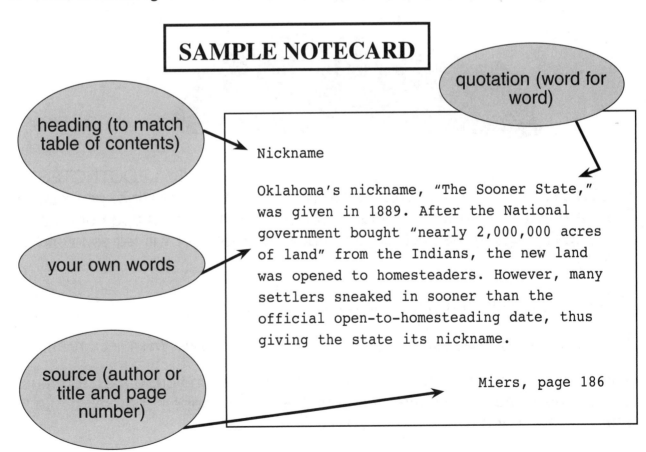

SAMPLE NOTECARD

heading (to match table of contents)

quotation (word for word)

your own words

source (author or title and page number)

Nickname

Oklahoma's nickname, "The Sooner State," was given in 1889. After the National government bought "nearly 2,000,000 acres of land" from the Indians, the new land was opened to homesteaders. However, many settlers sneaked in sooner than the official open-to-homesteading date, thus giving the state its nickname.

Miers, page 186

PREPARATION OF BIBLIOGRAPHY AND FOOTNOTES

Every report based on research needs to credit two things:

1. the sources used for the report

2. the words used for the report that were not your own

That is why a BIBLIOGRAPHY page and FOOTNOTES are needed in every research paper.

A **BIBLIOGRAPHY page** is an alphabetical listing of all the sources you used for your report. The page is at the end of your report and has the word BIBLIOGRAPHY written at the top. Here is an example.

BIBLIOGRAPHY

Brandt, Sue R. <u>Facts About The 50 States.</u> New York: Franklin Watts, Inc.,1979.

Collins, Howard. Personal Interview by Jesse Smith. Boise, Idaho: November 5, 1988.

<u>Rand McNally Book of The United States.</u> New York: Rand McNally and Company, 1962.

* BE SURE TO LIST ALL SOURCES USED IN YOUR BIBLIOGRAPHY.

If you copied anyone's words exactly, you must give credit in FOOTNOTES. A **FOOTNOTE** *tells who said what was in your quotation and where you found it.* There are two ways to write footnotes - at the bottom of each page or on a FOOTNOTE page at the back of your report. Your teacher will tell you which way to do it.

Here is an example of a single footnote.

   [1] Brandt, Sue R. <u>Facts About The 50 States</u> (New York: Franklin Watts, Inc., 1979), p.13.

(The number 1 indicates that this is the first quotation in your paper. You must also put the same number after the quotation in your paper. The next quote would have a 2, the next a 3, and so on. See page 11.)

* ALL FOOTNOTE SOURCES MUST ALSO BE IN YOUR BIBLIOGRAPHY.

QUOTATIONS AND PARAPHRASING

QUOTATIONS are words that are copied exactly from a source. Quotations are always enclosed in quotation marks.

"Maine was part of Massachusetts until its admission to the Union as a separate state."[1]

PARAPHRASING is how you write information from a source in your own words.

Until Maine became a state in the Union, it was part of Massachusetts.

Practice paraphrasing these quotes.

☆ "Florida's location gives it warm winters, and the surrounding water usually keeps it from becoming excessively hot in summer."[2]

_____

_____

_____

☆ "In 1880, when Chester A. Arthur became President upon the death of James A. Garfield, Vermont saw its first native son reach the White House."[3]

_____

_____

_____

☆ "Kentucky was part of Virginia until admitted as a state."[4]

_____

_____

_____

[1] Brandt, Sue R. Facts About The 50 States (New York: Franklin Watts, Inc., 1979), p.13.

[2] Rand McNally Book of the United States (New York: Rand McNally and Company,1962), p.48.

[3] Miers, Earl Schenck. Our Fifty States (New York: Grosset and Dunlap, 1961), p.29.

[4] Brandt, p. 13.

FACT AND OPINION

When you write a research paper, you must be very careful to stick to the FACTS. A research paper is written to give people INFORMATION that is true or can be proven true.

FACT – information that can be proven true.

OPINION – information that cannot be proven true.

Label these sentences as FACT or OPINION.

1. _____   Oregon has many lakes.

2. _____   Hawaii has the most beautiful islands in the world.

3. _____   Pennsylvania was one of the thirteen original states.

4. _____   Arkansas has mineral springs which can cure any illness.

5. _____   Virginia was the site of the first permanent English settlement in the New World.

6. _____   Michigan's shape is made by lakes.

7. _____   Texas is an oil-producing state.

8. _____   Iowa became a state in 1846.

9. _____   New York is an active center for art, music, and the theater.

10. _____   California has the lowest point in the nation — Death Valley.

At the end of your report, you may write opinions you have about your selected state, but you MUST make it clear that they are YOUR opinions.

REFERENCE BOOKS

A good place to begin the information search for your report is in a REFERENCE book. A **REFERENCE BOOK** *gives you general information about your subject.*

Reference books include encyclopedias, dictionaries, almanacs, atlas, and other books of general information.

Reference books are found in the reference section of the library. This section may be identified by the word REFERENCE, the Dewey Decimal System numbers 000-099, or both.

☆ When writing a bibliography card from a reference book, follow this format:

---

name of reference book_____

_____ (underlined)

author's name _____ (if given)

topic or subtitle (if given) _____

_____ (in quotation marks)

volume number or letter_____

publishing location _____

publishing company _____

copyright date _____

pages of useful information _____

total pages _____

☆ When transferring this information to the BIBLIOGRAPHY page of your report, follow this format:

Author's name (last name first). Article, "Title of Reference Book" (underlined).Volume _____(number or letter). Publishing location: Publishing Company, copyright date, article pages.

☆ When transferring this information to a FOOTNOTE, follow this format:

Author's name (first name first), "Article," Title of Reference Book (underlined), Volume _____.(Publishing location: Publishing Company, copyright date,p._____. (page or pages the quotation came from).

NON-FICTION BOOKS

After you have learned general information about your subject from reference books, you can find specific information in NON-FICTION books.

NON-FICTION books *are books that are true.* They have many facts in them about specific areas of interest. For example, you could find a non-fiction book about state history, national parks, or state birds!

Non-fiction books are arranged in the library according to Dewey Decimal System numbers. The most helpful areas for you in your report research would be **300-399 Social Science** and **900-999 History.**

☆ When writing a bibliography card from a non-fiction book, follow this format:

Author's name _____

title _____

_____ (underlined)

publishing location _____

publishing company _____

copyright date _____

call number _____

pages of useful information _____

total pages _____

☆ When transferring this information to the BIBLIOGRAPHY page of your report, follow this format.

Author's Name (last name first). Title (underlined). Publishing location: Publishing Company, copyright date.

☆ When transferring this information to a FOOTNOTE, follow this format:

[1] Author's Name (first name first), <u>Title</u> (underlined) (Publishing location: Publishing Company, copyright date), p._____ (page or pages the quotation came from).

PERIODICALS

Another source of information for your report are **PERIODICALS**. *PERIODICALS give you current information about your subject because they are published often, at regular intervals, such as weekly or monthly.*

Types of periodicals include magazines, daily newspapers, pamphlets, brochures, and other frequently published materials.

Periodicals are found in the newspaper and magazine section of the library. Other helpful periodicals may also be found in the Vertical File. *The Reader's Guide To Periodical Literature*, located in the Reference section of the library, can tell you if any magazine articles have been written about your subject.

☆ When writing a bibliography card from a periodical, follow this format:

author's name _____

article title _____

_____ (in quotation marks)

periodical title_____

_____ (underlined)

volume number _____

date of periodical _____

pages of useful information _____

total pages _____

☆ When transferring this information to the BIBLIOGRAPHY page of your report, follow this format:

Author's Name (last name first). "Article Title," (in quotation marks). Periodical Title (underlined), Volume number (date of periodical), page or pages of article.

☆ When transferring this information to a FOOTNOTE, follow this format:

[1] Author's Name (first name first), "Article Title," Periodical Title, Volume number (date of periodical), p._____.

INTERVIEWS

A great source of firsthand information about the subject of your report can be found in an INTERVIEW. **An INTERVIEW** *is a structured conversation with a person who is knowledgeable about your topic.*

Interviews can be scheduled with people who have lived in or traveled to your chosen area. Just remember to keep facts and opinions clearly identified.

Your role in an interview is to set up clear questions that pertain to the individual areas in your report. If done well, a good interview can add needed information and a personal touch to your report.

☆ When writing a bibliography card from an interview, follow this format:

name of interviewee _____

_____

interview location _____

_____

interview date _____

_____

name of interviewer _____

_____

☆ When transferring this information to the BIBLIOGRAPHY page of your report, follow this format:

Interviewee's Name (last name first). Interviewed by _____.
Interview location, interview date and time.

☆ When transferring this information to a FOOTNOTE, follow this format:

[1] Interviewee's Name (first name first), interviewed by _____
(Interview location, interview date and time).

INTEREST INVENTORY

1. Draw a box around the name of the state in which you live.

2. Use a blue crayon to color the boxes next to the states you are very interested in learning more about.

3. Use a red crayon to color the circles next to the states you have visited. If you have traveled through your own state, color that circle also.

☐ ○ Alabama   ☐ ○ Louisiana   ☐ ○ Ohio

☐ ○ Alaska   ☐ ○ Maine   ☐ ○ Oklahoma

☐ ○ Arizona   ☐ ○ Maryland   ☐ ○ Oregon

☐ ○ Arkansas   ☐ ○ Massachusetts   ☐ ○ Pennsylvania

☐ ○ California   ☐ ○ Michigan   ☐ ○ Rhode Island

☐ ○ Colorado   ☐ ○ Minnesota   ☐ ○ South Carolina

☐ ○ Connecticut   ☐ ○ Mississippi   ☐ ○ South Dakota

☐ ○ Delaware   ☐ ○ Missouri   ☐ ○ Tennessee

☐ ○ Florida   ☐ ○ Montana   ☐ ○ Texas

☐ ○ Georgia   ☐ ○ Nebraska   ☐ ○ Utah

☐ ○ Hawaii   ☐ ○ Nevada   ☐ ○ Vermont

☐ ○ Idaho   ☐ ○ New Hampshire   ☐ ○ Virginia

☐ ○ Illinois   ☐ ○ New Jersey   ☐ ○ Washington

☐ ○ Indiana   ☐ ○ New Mexico   ☐ ○ West Virginia

☐ ○ Iowa   ☐ ○ New York   ☐ ○ Wisconsin

☐ ○ Kansas   ☐ ○ North Carolina   ☐ ○ Wyoming

☐ ○ Kentucky   ☐ ○ North Dakota

Choose three states that you would be interested in researching for your state report. Put them in your order of preference.

1._____   2. _____   3. _____

INTRODUCTION TO A STATE REPORT

A state report is a report for which you research information about your selected state and put this information into a written and pictorial format.

The pages which follow are guidelines for this type of report. You may use these pages in two ways.

1. They can be the actual pages of your report, completed by your research.

2. They can serve as springboards for your own ideas on how best to organize and complete your report, with you creating each page in your own words and style.

Not all of the pages will be applicable to your state. Use what applies for your particular report. Similarly, not all of the areas you would like to cover may be represented by the pages given. Create new pages for these areas! Here are some ideas you might use.

☆ State animal

☆ State tree

☆ Motto

☆ Fashions

☆ Customs

☆ Ethnic make-up

☆ Comparison of past and present resources

☆ Historical notes behind flag or other symbols

☆ Additional maps, graphs, and charts about specific areas such as geography areas and their climate

☆ Religions

☆ Elaboration on native plants and animals

☆ State character

☆ Etc.

We hope you enjoy researching and writing your report. It can open your mind to the uniqueness and beauty in each state.

CHECKLIST

Are you ready to begin your state report? Before you begin, read this list. Check the things on the list you can answer with "yes."

- [ ] Has your teacher approved your state choice?

- [ ] Do you understand any special rules your teacher has given you for writing your state report? Write the rules here.

_____

_____

_____

- [ ] Do you know the due dates for your project(s) and paper? Write the dates.

    projects(s) _____

    paper _____

- [ ] Has your teacher given you any checkpoint due dates to see the progress of your report? Write the dates.

    bibliography _____ notecards _____

    outline or table of contents_____

    maps _____ first draft _____

    other_____

- [ ] Do you have more than one source of information for your report? How many?

- [ ] Do you have all the materials you need to begin writing your report?

- [ ] Will you remember to be as neat as you can be in your writing and drawing?

If you checked all the items on this list, you' re ready to begin writing your state report!

MY
STATE
REPORT

on

_____

by

_____

_____

MY STATE REPORT

ON

_____

Table of
Contents

WHAT'S IN A NAME?

Here is an explanation of how my state got its name.

_____

_____

_____

_____

This is the nickname that my state has been given.

_____

Here is an explanation of how my state got its nickname.

_____

_____

_____

_____

_____

_____

_____

_____

_____

LOCATION OF STATE

I have colored my state blue and labeled all of its neighbors.

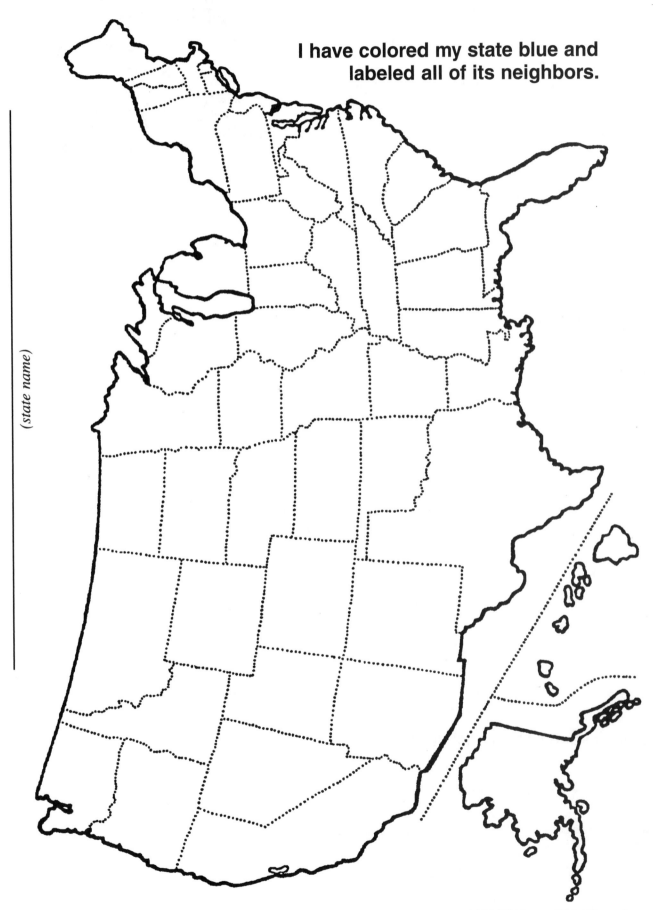

(state name)

EARLY HISTORICAL FACTS

Listed below is the early history of my state.

First known inhabitants _____

_____

_____

_____

Exploration _____

_____

_____

_____

Settlement _____

_____

_____

Colonial and/or territorial days _____

_____

_____

_____

STATEHOOD HISTORY

_____

is the _____state

in the United States.

Here is the history of how it became a state.

_____

_____

_____

_____

_____

_____

_____

_____

_____

_____

_____

_____

_____

_____

Physical Features

of

_____

My state has _____ main land regions.

Each region is described below.

_____

_____

_____

_____

_____

_____

_____

The highest point in the state is _____

_____ at _____

The lowest point in the state is _____at _____

The area of the state is _____

It ranks_____ in size among the states.

A PHYSICAL MAP of my state follows this page.

POLITICAL FEATURES

of

_____

☆ The population of my state is _____ people

as of this date: _____

☆ There are _____ counties in the state.

The largest county in size is _____ ,

measuring _____ square miles.

The largest county in population is _____

_____ with _____ people.

☆ The five largest cities and their populations are:

_____   _____ people

_____   _____ people

_____   _____ people

_____   _____ people

_____   _____ people

as of this date _____

☆ The major highways in the state are

_____

_____

_____

A POLITICAL MAP of my state follows this page.

STATE FLAG

STATE SEAL

STATE BIRD

_____

STATE FLOWER

_____

STATE LICENSE PLATE

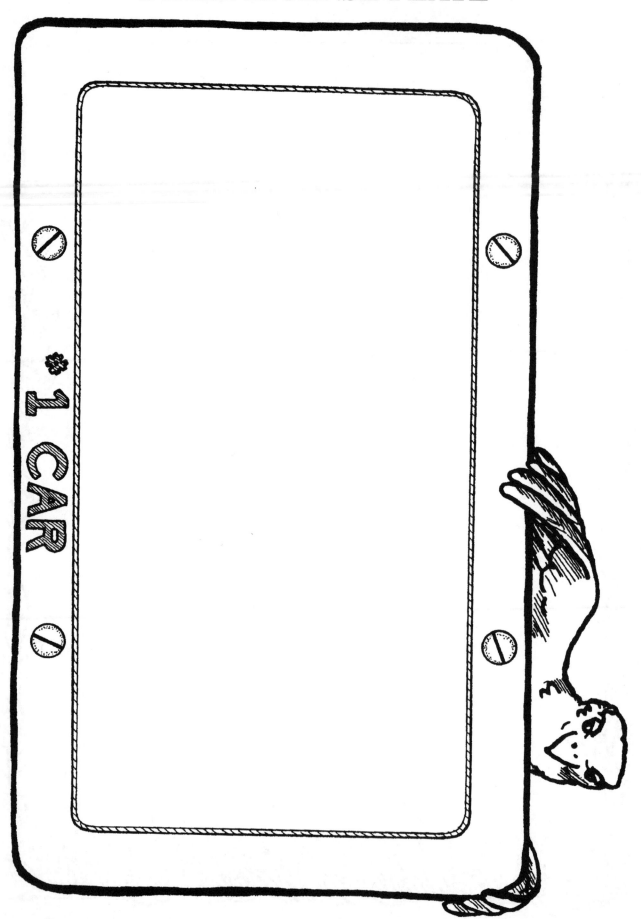

1 CAR

SONG OR POEM ABOUT STATE

WEATHER

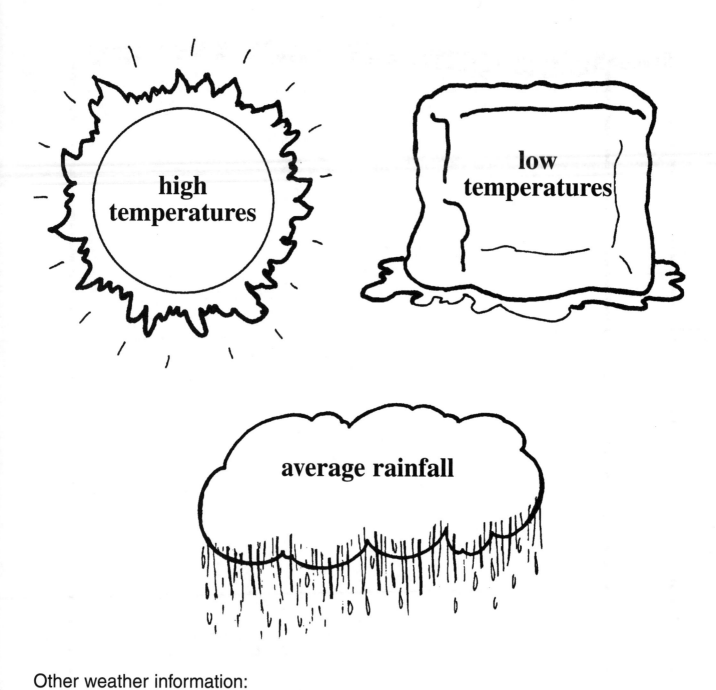

high
temperatures

low
temperatures

average rainfall

Other weather information:

_____

_____

_____

_____

RESOURCES

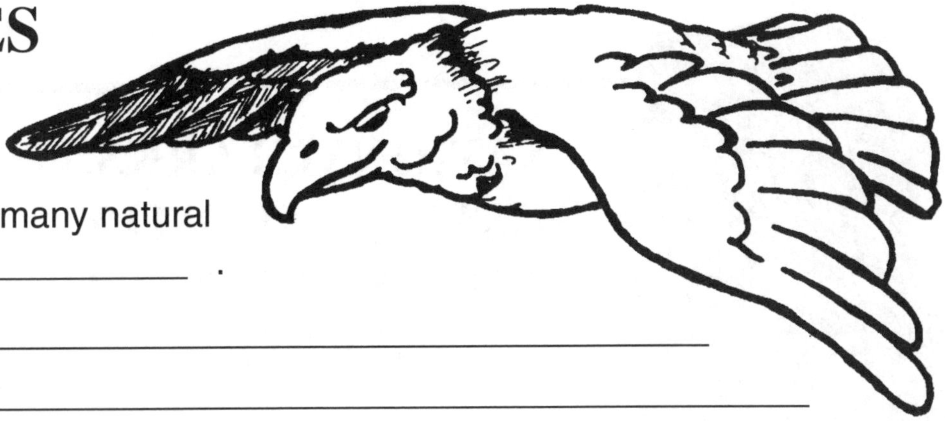

Listed below are the many natural
resources of_____ .

☆ Water: _____

_____

_____

☆ Soil: _____

_____

_____

☆ Minerals: _____

_____

_____

☆ Plant Life:_____

_____

_____

☆ Animal Life: _____

_____

_____

_____

_____

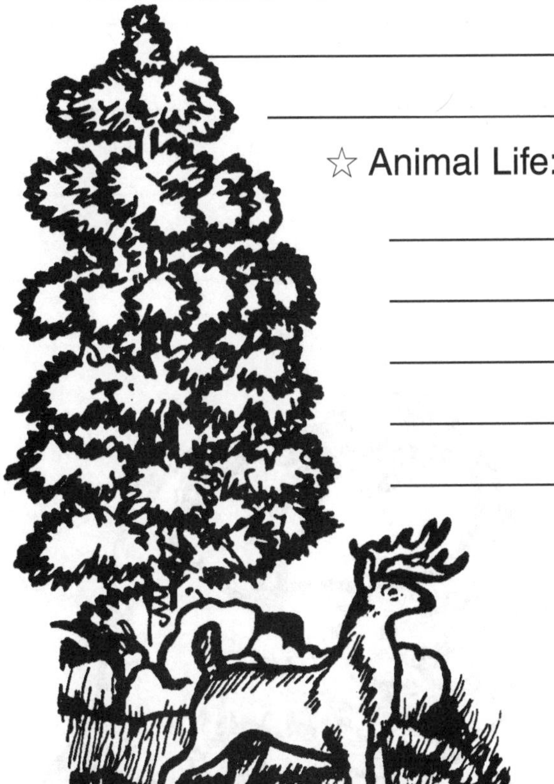

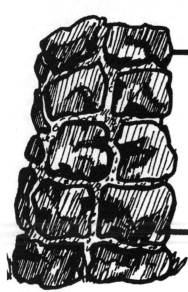

NATIONAL PARKS, HISTORICAL SITES, and OTHER POINTS OF INTEREST

Listed below are the national parks, historical parks, battlefields, memorials, monuments, historic sites, preserves, and other areas administered by the National Park Service.

_____

_____

_____

_____

_____

_____

_____

_____

_____

_____

_____

FAMOUS PEOPLE

Listed below are famous residents of my state and what they did to become famous

☆ _____

_____

_____

☆ _____

_____

_____

☆ _____

_____

_____

☆ _____

_____

_____

☆ _____

_____

_____

GOVERNMENT

Here are facts about the government of _____ .

☆ NATIONAL GOVERNMENT

The participants in the United States Congress from my state number
_____ U.S. Senator(s) and
_____ U.S. Representative(s).

My state has _____ electoral vote(s).

☆ STATE GOVERNMENT

My state is headed by _____ as Governor.

The make-up of the state legislature is as follows:

_____

_____

_____

_____

☆ LOCAL GOVERNMENT

The local government of my state can be described as follows:

_____

_____

_____

_____

☆ OTHER FACTS RELATING TO GOVERNMENT

_____

_____

_____

_____

_____

EDUCATION

_____ established its public schools systems

in _____ . State law requires children between _____

and _____ years of age to attend school.

☆ Here are other facts about education in my state.

_____

_____

_____

_____

These statistics relate to enrollment and teachers.

Number of local school districts _____

Total public school enrollment_____

Pupils per teacher _____

Number of classroom teachers _____

Teacher's average pay_____

Total private school enrollment _____

☆ A listing of universities and colleges and
   their locations follows this page.

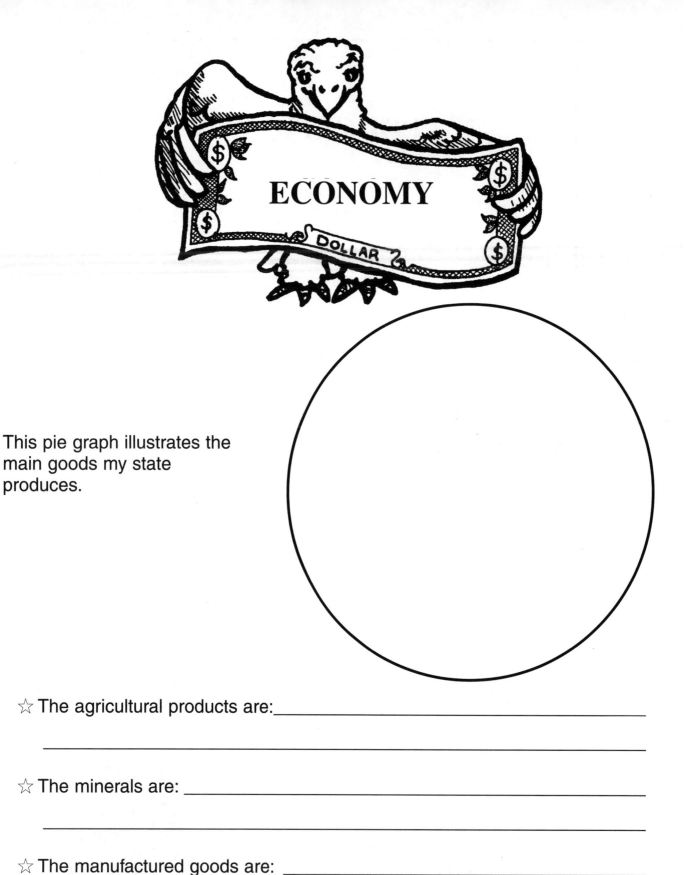

ECONOMY

This pie graph illustrates the main goods my state produces.

☆ The agricultural products are: _____

_____

☆ The minerals are: _____

_____

☆ The manufactured goods are: _____

_____

A **PRODUCT MAP** of the location of the leading areas for agricultural, mineral, and manufactured goods production follows this page.

POPULATION GROWTH AND DENSITY

On the left side of the graphs below write in the population for each of the five years. On the bottom of the graph identify each year. Then, fill in your bar graph.

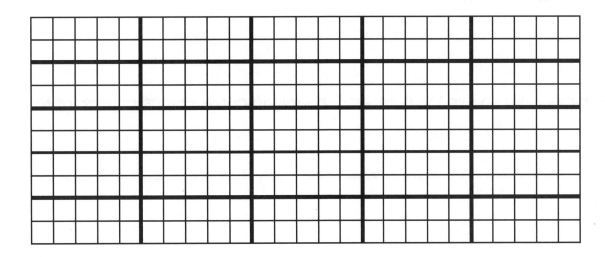

years:_____   _____   _____   _____   _____

Here is a bar graph comparing the population density of my state in three different years.

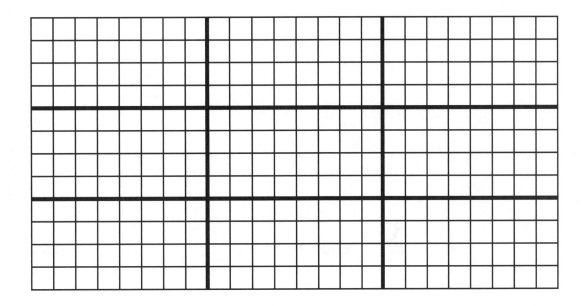

years:_____   _____   _____

EMPLOYMENT

In the year _____ there were

_____ people employed

in the state of

_____ .

This pictograph shows the number of people in certain types of jobs for the

year _____ .

| |
| |

one equals _____ people

VISITOR'S GUIDE

Listed below are areas in my state that would be interesting to visit. Next to each place is its location and a description of what it is that makes the place interesting.

_____

_____

_____

_____

_____

_____

_____

_____

_____

_____

_____

_____

_____

_____

OPINIONS

Before writing this report, I had opinions about the state I chose. This is what I thought.

_____

_____

_____

_____

_____

After completing this report, I have new opinions about the state I chose. This is what I think.

_____

_____

_____

_____

_____

_____

_____

_____

_____

BIBLIOGRAPHY

_____

_____

_____

_____

_____

_____

_____

_____

_____

_____

_____

_____

_____

_____

_____

_____

_____

PROJECT IDEAS

A PROJECT helps you understand more about your state. It can also be very interesting for other people to see.

Your teacher will tell you how many projects you will need to accompany your state report.

Here are **some** ideas.

- ☆ Construct a timeline of historical events.

- ☆ Create a variety of state maps, including a relief map, a resources map with attached figures, and a large political map.

- ☆ Make a diorama or other three-dimensional representation of a state place of interest.

- ☆ Research a famous person from the state and write a biography.

- ☆ Create a play or puppet show about a moment in the state's history.

- ☆ Find and communicate with a pen pal from the state.

- ☆ Assemble a travel brochure, pamphlet, or poster that would "sell" the specialness of the state.

- ☆ Prepare and serve a food enjoyed by state residents.

- ☆ Dress for a state fashion show—past and/or present.

- ☆ Construct graphs that show specific points about the state.

- ☆ Collect newspaper articles about your state and put together a state scrapbook.

- ☆ Devise a test for the readers of your state report.

EVALUATION

☆ I enjoyed/did not enjoy doing a state report because

_____

_____

_____

_____

☆ The most interesting thing I learned about my state:

_____

_____

☆ The part of my report that was the hardest to do:

_____

_____

☆ The part of my report that was the most fun to do:

_____

_____

☆ Areas in which I felt I did a good job:

_____

_____

☆ Things I would do differently if I could do my report over:

_____

_____

☆ Advice I would give people who are about to begin a state report:

_____

☆ Other comments:

_____

TRAVEL PLANS

You have had an opportunity to hear or read about the states your classmates have researched. Based on what you have learned, which state would you like to visit most?

_____

Complete this travel ticket to the state you have just selected.

TRAVEL TICKET

The state I would most like to

see is...

_____

It appeals to me because...

_____

_____

_____

_____

ADMIT _____

TO _____

FROM THIS DATE _____

TO THIS DATE _____